Citizen 2.0

A Practical Guide to Participating in an
Always On Globally Connected Society

C. Ethan Blue

DEDICATION

Dedicated in loving memory to my late Grandpa, Boyd Elliott; whose pursuit of higher education and love for laughter inspired me to chase my goals and laugh at myself when I fell miserably short of them.

Also, none of my achievements would be possible without the amazing experiences I have had with friends and family both past and present. You are always in my thoughts.

CONTENTS

Prologue   vii

1 It's Not How It Used To Be   1

2 You're Wrong!   23

3 Your Brand   40

4 Your Participation   72

5 Your Knowledge   95

PROLOGUE

Citizenship is a funny word. Not funny like Louis C.K. funny, it's more of a funny because it can mean different things depending on its context type of funny. In its most basic form, citizenship means that you are a member of a community. In a deeper way, it can refer to your rights and responsibilities as a member of that community.

Rights and responsibilities vary depending on what community you are a citizen of, but what happens when we all become a member of the same community?

The rapid worldwide adoption of the internet is bringing questions such as these to the forefront. Citizen 2.0 attempts to tackle some of these questions with my own personal insights and what may or may not be considered humor.

If you have any questions or comments, they may be directed to Citizen2.0@cebcorps.com

Enjoy!

CHAPTER 1: IT'S NOT HOW IT USED TO BE - ABANDONING BIAS IN A SHRINKING SOCIETY

I didn't get Internet access at home until I was a teenager. That may seem young to many of you reading this book; hell, it seems young to me, but access has become so ubiquitous that now it's hard to find any sort of child in the US who does not utilize the Internet in some way.

When we first signed up for service, we were promised blazing fast 56k speeds that could download a 640x480 picture in less than five minutes. Poppycock, I cried! Such claims are certainly no more than science fiction. At the time I had no idea what 640x480 meant, nor did I have any context of what 56k was. All I knew is that I would be able to reenact my smooth pick-up line that I developed in the AOL chat rooms at my buddy Jared's house: "Prevch presents a rose to all the ladies in the room." (Prevch is my online name that I stole from my satellite remote, by the way.)

Back when chat rooms weren't considered the creepy cesspool of online predators, such a romantic gesture generally got at least a moderate response. For every "what a loser" there was like five "Awww, that's so romantic's." Before alcohol even got its opportunity to try, the power of the Internet drew out my inner Casanova.

MSNBC's *To Catch a Predator* has somewhat sullied the rose colored lens with which I tend to look back on my early chat room days. 13 year old Prevch was unaware that many of the young "ladies" he was swooning were likely very, very creepy old men. You know what, let's just say they were all 13 year old girls.

After convincing my parents that access to the Internet would be educationally beneficial and that the magic that made computers talk to the outside world didn't mark the coming of the anti-Christ, (unless you consider pop-up ads and spam email evil incarnate in which case I owe my parent's an apology) they finally agreed to sign up.

I remember watching the installation technician installing a new phone jack in our home office. I'm certain he was sick of me by the time he left. He was bamboozled with questions like "what does that do?" and "are you sure that's hooked up right?" Bear in mind that, at this point in my life, my training in the information technology field was nil. It's just that I had a lot riding on this install. If this guy did it right, I would be able to spark notes my *Great Gatsby* homework and present a chat rose to a creepy, old man by supper. It's sort of like that weird control freak airplane effect people get. When I fly and we hit turbulents, I white knuckle my seat and think "You know, I really should be flying this plane right now" my current aviation training, zero.

After what felt like a short eternity, the install tech finished up and I was able to begin surfing the tumultuous waves of the interwebs. Much to my dismay, upon attempting to go to Yahoo's website, I noticed a red X in the lower right hand corner of my computer screen. Apparently the combined strain of my nigh giddy aura and someone in the house picking up the telephone was enough to obliterate a perfectly good internet connection. Many of us forget, or simply don't appreciate it, how good we have it now. So, for the sake of sour grapes, since I'm mad at every child who never had to live through such an ordeal, let's compare how one surfs the web now to how one surfed the web then:

Now

Step 1: Turn on the computer and monitor.

Step 2: Open Internet Browser of choice.

Step 3: Surf.

Then

Step 1: Turn on the computer (This could take a long time depending on the circumstances) and if you had an old CRT monitor that needed to warm up you could tack some time on. This also doesn't take into account the recuperation time from the jolt of static electricity that was sent through your body when you touched the computer screen since your stocking feet grazed the carpet on the way there.

Step 2: Navigate to network properties section on your computer and find the phone icon representing a dial-up internet connection and open it.

Step 3: Check to make sure that there is a phone number in the number box. If not and you don't remember it, call customer support. If you don't know their number, look it up in the phone book.

Step 4: Call customer support and speak with a thickly accented gentleman who tells you his name is Bob Smith. Get placed on hold.

Step 5: Watch *Golden Girls* re-runs while on hold with customer support. Sophia is the best. I'm naming my kid Sophia.

Step 6: Have sister pull out phone cord from wall and get disconnected from customer support.

Step 7: Wait for sister to finish babbling on the phone.

Step 8: Call customer support back, ask for Bob Smith.

Step 9: Watch *Golden Girls* re-runs while waiting for Bob. Blanch, you floozy.

Step 10: Exchange pleasantries with Bob. Get appropriate dial-in number.

Step 11: Go back to computer and type in dial-in number in appropriate place. Click connect.

Step 12: Listen to the sultry serenade of a US Robotics modem attempt to dial in and make a connection. For those not privy to what a dial-up modem sounds like, I suggest you look it up on your fancy always-on, practically instantaneous internet connection. It starts off with a dial tone, then sort of sounds like an auto-tuned robotic cow mooing, but the cow is in some sort of emotional distress as expressed with yells at different pitches that are doused in static with the occasional sprinkling of a ding like noise, brand specific of course, all set to a 4/4 time signature. I always knew if that [expletive deleted] hit B flat on the 1 in the second measure, it wasn't going to connect.

Step 13: Connection Failed. Try to reconnect.

Step 14: Connect at 14.4k and surf the net so slow you are forced to call customer support.

Step 15: Call customer support, ask for Bob.

Step 16: Explain to Bob that my 56k modem is connecting at 14.4. Bob replies that the 56k speed is hypothetical and that connection speeds vary based on many circumstances.

Step 17: Hang up and reconnect at 14.4.

Step 18: Watch *Golden Girls* re-runs while waiting for Yahoo. I wonder if there really is a St. Olaf, Minnesota. Wish I could look it up on a functional internet connection.

Step 19: Walk back into computer room and realize you lost the connection.

Step 20: Call customer support, ask for Bob.

Step 21: Bob gives modem string to add into dial-up network

connection property and tells me to test that. Bear in mind that I am forced to hang up in order to test if the modem string worked, it's not like I can tell Bob to hold.

Step 22: Connect at 28.8. Grind through surfing session and pray for a better tomorrow.

These were trying times, indeed. Cell phones were uncommon. No one in my household had one and even if they had, we didn't have the infrastructure to support it. In other words, the only way for me to connect to the internet and fulfill my destiny of presenting digital roses to strangers was via the only means of instant communication my family had to the larger outside world; a landline phone which was monopolized by my tyrannical sister.

There was a point in my life when I was actually convinced that my teenage sister had a phone growing out of her head. Who could she possibly be talking to for such an obscene amount of time? I have no idea how many friends my sister had in high school, but for someone as grouchy as she was, (she's a much nicer person now) I can't imagine it would be a sum large enough to warrant permanently affixing a cordless phone to her face. How are they not running out of things to talk about? Yes, Brenda and Dylan from *Beverly Hills 90210* broke up for the umpteenth time, how many different ways can one express their disbelief? Such trifles sullied my digital exploration.

When I did get to surf, I felt like a pioneer exploring new territory. I wasn't a patient child, but I was painfully curious and the allure of the knowledge I could seek out on the Internet was too great to resist. Granted, most of that knowledge was related to video games, but at least I was seeking. I started viewing web pages' source code to try and learn how they were put together. I didn't understand what the vast majority of the code meant, so I would just download the source to my local machine and mess around with it to see what would happen. Like a sandbox, I built, destroyed and experimented; and, most importantly, I learned.

To my parents' credit, I think they noticed how much of an interest I had in computers and finally caved when I started asking for a second phone line for Christmas. Once the second phone line came in, I became somewhat of a recluse. It didn't matter much, my buddies always hung out at my house anyway, so I still had a healthy social life, but I was addicted to the net, despite its drudgingly slow nature.

Then, one fateful day, my buddy Jared told me that his grandparents had cable internet. Internet that worked through the cable line, did not interfere with the cable TV, did not occupy a phone line and loaded web pages, even ones with pictures, virtually instantaneously. It was like I had found an elusive unicorn galloping through a magical forest. I immediately called the cable company to find out if such wonderment actually existed. Ginny, the lady from the cable company, confirmed that it did, but that it was not available in my area. After hearing those words, I collapsed inside. My heart had not gone through such complex emotions since Ultimate Warrior bested Hulk Hogan at *Wrestlemania VI*. Suddenly, Ginny said "but" and I automatically went to visions of Ginny meeting me at night in a back alley lit only by a single flood light on the side of a worn down brick building wearing a full length trench coat that housed a special piece of technical equipment. Of course, I had a full pinstripe suit with a briefcase and fedora. I would say "You got the stuff?" and she would reply "Maybe. You got the money?" I would continue "I don't show you the money until you show me the stuff." Our mafia-like transaction would end with me walking away with a secret gizmo that allowed me to navigate the web at Mach 5. What really happened is considerably less exciting than the scenario that played out in my brain.

Ginny finished our conversation by saying "we are always expanding our services, so check back periodically." Ginny didn't define "periodically" and I'm guessing she later came to regret that decision. Weekly, for the next 9 months, I called Ginny to discuss the expansion of cable Internet into my area. I knew I was calling too much when she started using my full name. I defended myself by explaining how difficult it was for a teenage boy to look up pictures of Lucy Lawless, TV's *Xena the Warrior Princess*, in a bikini on a dial-up modem. She didn't seem to share my concerns. Maybe had I said Fabio, I would have gotten a little more sympathy.

Eventually, on what I'm sure was a milestone day for Ginny since I know it was for me, she was able to tell me that cable internet service was available in my area. When I told her I wasn't interested she said "You're getting it. When would you like us to come set it up?" Apparently, she saw right through my ruse.

Ginny proceeded to tell me that Mitch, the installation tech, would be out to my house to install service sometime between next Wednesday and Friday between 1am and 10pm. Ok, that might be a bit of an exaggeration, but it was some time in the next week or so. Lucky for them, I didn't have any pressing matters to attend to.

When I was a kid, a few times each year at school we would have an early release day. The final school bell rang around noon and we were free to go. Usually, on early release days, I would hang out with my buddy, Brett. I would go to his house or he would come to mine and we would fill our afternoons with educational programming; and by educational programming, I am referring to Nintendo. For some reason, those school days seemed to last twice as long as a standard day. I'm sure it was just because I was excited to do something fun, but man were the mornings painful. A similar phenomenon occurred to me while waiting for high speed internet service. Like living in some weird alternate dimension, time seemed to actually slow down.

When Mitch finally arrived at my door, I had no time for pleasantries. I marched him directly to the computer and said "It's go time." When he tried to make small talk with me, I limited my responses to one word answers. Mitch: "So, you like computers?" Me: "Yeah." Mitch: "What's your favorite class at school?" Me: "Gym." This was very much out of character. I'm generally a chatty person, but like a drug addict, I could focus only on my binary fix; today, I was chasing that DogPile dragon.

Mitch connected to the Internet and did a speed test. I had never seen anything more illustrious, nor have I since. He actually mentioned that my speed, while good, was just barely on the slow side. I told Mitch the advertised speeds were simply hypothetical and that my speeds may vary depending on a number of factors..........wow. I was so anxious to get online that I actually used Bob Smith's customer-calming-response on an installation tech. I then proceeded to tell him "good day". In other words, get out. When he responded that there was one other thing he wanted to test before he left, I can't remember my exact response, but it might as well have been "I said good day!" Again, totally uncharacteristic of me. I was now connected to the internet with an always-on, broadband connection. The world is my smorgasbord. Bon Appétit!

Since that glorious day, I haven't looked back. Unfortunately for me and my loving family, I can't say that I came up with some brilliant dotcom or made millions of dollars from a snazzy website. No, my gain was much less financial than it was experimental and educational. I learned so much from simply looking up questions I had and reading, contemplating and discussing those thoughts with others. Granted, most of my questions related to video games, (or Xena in a bikini as it were) but people's responses were often sprinkled with thoughts and views from other parts of their lives. The occasional *BattleToads* conversation referring to

Pimple's unplayability due to his abduction, would eventually lead to the US's policy on negotiating with terrorists. Hence, the bias-blanket-thought-pattern that I quilted from the fabric of friends and family with which I insulated my life and curled up in at night, was under construction. Don't get me wrong, the thoughts, feelings and experiences that I have gained from friends and family are imperative to who I am as a person. Those people and Little Debbie have made me the man I am today.

Before I continue, I should mention that the following portion of this book discusses parts of my own personal journey including some of my experiences with religion. Please bear in mind that this is a reflection of my experience and not a judgment, endorsement or condemnation of anyone else's beliefs.

I grew up in a conservative household. Church was attended every Sunday and decisions were, more or less, black and white. There was good and there was evil; so be a good believer or else. That's what I took away from the lessons anyway. In retrospect, I suppose most people have a somewhat similar system, be it wrapped in the veil of a religion or otherwise. The non-secular "Be good or you're grounded" is basically the same as "Be good and accept Jesus or you're grounded AND going to hell", conceptually anyway. I actually appreciate the simplicity of it. It's difficult for people to understand complex gray areas, especially children.

My natural disposition was of a relatively well behaved child, but the fear-of-God and my mother's wrath with yard sticks was usually enough to keep me in line if I was having a moment. As I got older, I began to question the lessons that I had previously been taught and the beliefs I held onto. I think that's natural for most people in all aspects of their life, not just religion. Church taught me so many good things. Loving your neighbor, helping the less fortunate, building community, but there were things that just didn't jive with my mojo. This doubting process was an incredibly confusing and upsetting process for me. Emotional growing pains if you will. I was riddled with guilt from the internal struggle between my upbringing and my own self-discovery.

My fancy new internet connection allowed me to look up questions like "How could Noah fit all those animals on his boat?" and "How did Jonah survive in the belly of a whale?" Usually my searches left me just as confused as when I started. I've come to learn that people believe what they want to believe and will justify it by any means necessary.

I actually listened to a radio program that interviewed some psychologists and brain researchers about why people believe what they do. Many of the answers were what you would expect. They discussed things like where the person grew up, what their family was like, who they spent time with, their socioeconomic status and their own natural disposition as factors. For many of us, if an idea or finding does not pair well with our own bias, we simply disregard it. Researchers found that in many cases, even if someone was presented with hard evidence that was contrarian to their beliefs, they may temporarily alter their thinking about the subject, but would ultimately revert to their previously held stance in a short period of time. Like my wife in a fight, she won't let a little thing like facts get in the way of her arguments.

I've certainly been guilty of this in the past. We probably all have. I assume it's a built-in coping mechanism. We need to convince ourselves that we are correct or live with the consequences that go along with accepting our fallibility which can be a hard pill to swallow.

The internet assisted me in changing my world perspective. Just the simple exposure to so many new concepts and ways of life helped me to further develop my views. The other thing that truly expanded my thinking was college.

Interestingly enough, I was never really in to school, save for gym class. Prisoner dodge ball for the win! I always just wanted to do my own thing. Fast forward to my adult life and here I am teaching college and with a passion for learning. Go figure. If I had to pick one thing in my life that I felt truly developed my brain, it would have to be college. I didn't like all of my classes; no, far from it. I did, however, enjoy meeting a lot of people from all over the world who had vastly different backgrounds and beliefs from that of my own. To hear and learn about their experiences was truly educational.

There were some classes that I liked, especially ones that were computer related. Professor Elena Bertozzi taught many of them and more than any other professor I have had, she taught me how to push myself. She was especially nasty when it came to writing. I can't tell you how many times this lady gave me back the papers that I turned in and told me to redo it. I told my buddy Collin, who was in class with me, that she had "Dissertation Diarrhea;" a condition that affects those who were forced to write a dissertation to complete their degree. Symptoms include being irritable from the work and stress that goes into a dissertation and dumping said pain and discomfort onto poor, unsuspecting undergraduates. Of course, I completely made all of that up. She was just trying to teach us how to write. She's actually a very cool person. I learned a lot from her and am truly thankful for that, but there was one class, totally unrelated to my major, that made quite an impact on me in terms of my perspective and that class was "World of Ideas."

World of Ideas was a gen-ed philosophy course that came in a few different flavors. If I remember correctly, the flavor I chose was "the human condition." This was an intensive three week romp that I took over winter break. The class discussed several different world religions and moral structures and the history behind them. Professor David Cartwright spoke with raspy fortitude as he delivered his lesson. The thing I loved about his teaching style was that no one had any idea what he believed.

Traditionally, an educator has a viewpoint and delivers a lesson with prejudices built in. Not Dr. Cartwright. One week he would play the role of a Christian who spoke about his religion as fact. The next, he was a Taoist who didn't concern himself with such trifles. Every role he played, he defended with appropriate conviction and relatively reasonable arguments. His portrayal helped me to better understand where people were coming from.

I don't study people or world religions, but his lessons helped me to view issues more holistically. What are all the angles? What are the consequences? Why would party A believe this and party B believe that? Why do both parties believe they are right? I truly believe that the education I have received has helped me to be a better citizen both in-person and online.

So here we are, in this big world separated by huge oceans, yet we are closer than ever. Now that the cables have been run, the internet has become a digital representation of a land lock. A true Pangaea. If you're old, take comfort in the fact that you'll be dead soon. For those of us who hopefully still have a decent amount of time left, strap in for a blitzkrieg of technological advancement and cultural change.

It's not how it used to be. Our forefathers could live generations totally isolated by the assumptions and prejudices passed onto them by their forefathers. It was easy. The only people they had to answer to were those they learned their opinions from. This is no longer so. Thoughts and opinions get placed on the net and processed by the masses and therein lies the magic. It's almost like a Euro effect. Europe has so many countries positioned so closely together that, even though each country has its own individual culture, they have almost no choice but to experience some of what their neighbors have to offer. Just think of how many Europeans are multilingual. Proximity led to absorption.

I refer to this phenomena as "digipangeaeological proximity." In other words, we all live in the same net neighborhood, so we better learn how to get along.

So how does one begin to abandon their own, long held biases? To steal Dr. Phil's catchphrase, "you can't change what you don't acknowledge." In other words, be cognoscente about your thoughts and feelings......like a Jedi. Most people don't actively think about what they think about.

I think it's important to ask yourself questions about why you feel how you feel.

Are you an atheist? Why? Have you ever attended church? Have you ever studied any religions or spoken to a person of faith?

Are you a devoutly religious person? How come? Did you come to the religion on your own or is that what you were taught? Is your religion based off of your geographical location? Have you ever spoken to someone of another faith about their beliefs? Have you ever spoken to an atheist to determine their reasons for not being religious?

Do you hate people from a certain race? Was this a learned behavior or did you have a bad experience?

Do you hate computers? Why? What do you know about them? Have you received any education on computers?

Do you love the color purple? What brought you to that conclusion? What experiences have you had with the color?

Do you like ice cream? This is a horrible example; ice cream is just downright awesome, discussion over.

My point is, I foresee the internet facilitating many more interactions with people we may or may not have come across via more traditional means. We need to be critical of our thoughts and cognoscente of our biases if we are going to live in a civil neighborhood.

Kevin Smith's movie, *Dogma* had some really great lines. Chris Rock played an apostle of the Christian God and spoke about how he recommended people have ideas instead of beliefs. He went on to explain that ideas are thoughts that can lead our lives, but they also can be malleable. Ideas can be rearranged, updated and modified without the need for violence. People fight and die for beliefs, but that does not necessarily make them valid.

This isn't my way of saying abandon all of your morals. Nor is it me saying that what you think or feel is wrong. No, what I'm saying is, for most of us, our popular biases/beliefs are going to slowly be eroded through natural societal progression and globalization. Honestly, I don't think that's a bad thing. I truly believe that the majority of people's default setting is one of cooperation. The more we become one people, the more we incorporate global sensibilities and ultimately become a stronger community. We have the responsibility to be a contributing citizen and part of that is being a good neighbor.

Chapter 1 practical recommendations:

1. Get broadband internet.

2. Take a world studies course.

3. Make friends with people who believe something totally different than you do.

4. Open your mind to new ideas.

5. Always question your thoughts and take time to reflect on them.

CHAPTER 2: YOU'RE WRONG! - EVERYONE ON THE INTERNET THINKS THEY ARE SMARTER THAN YOU

For those of us with significant others, the concept of being persistently wrong is not a foreign one. For those of us lucky enough to be unattached, it might take some getting used. I'm a big supporter of people participating online in a safe and productive manner. Name your interest and almost certainly you can find someone online that has similar tastes.

I watched a documentary on human sexuality and one of the interviewees said that what turns him on are balloons. No, not flying over the countryside in a romantic hot air balloon. Literally, just normal balloons. They showed him in a room full of them and he looked super happy. He also enjoyed popping the balloons through various means. He would pop a balloon and get this huge smile on his face. I don't know about you, but I think this guy has it all figured out. No fancy dates and expensive dinners, just a trip to the drugstore to pick up a pack of balloons and he's set for the weekend. He did mention, however that he felt very isolated. Let's face it, you're not just going to go to the bar and ask potential suitors if they'd like to come back to your place and pop some balloons. His feeling of isolation led him to the Internet to seek out others with similar interests and to his surprise and mine, he's not the only one! He even found a party that he could go to and blow up balloons with other people! So, whether you are turned on by exploding balloons or just enjoy baseball, someone out there shares your interest.

Forums and social media are pretty common places for people to come together and wax idiotic about all manner of things, but it seems to frequently relate to cats for some unknown reason. Regardless, if you're seeking out a discussion, these are good places to start.

Most of the people that I have had any sort of meaningful interaction with on the internet have been relatively easy to get along with. That being said, every crevice of the net has someone that will do anything they can to try and make you crazy. These people are often referred to as trolls. Do you like the color blue? The troll watching you hates it, it's ugly and so are you. Do you like TV's latest cop drama? That's because you're a dummy and you wouldn't know good entertainment if it hit you in the face.

Here are some common signs that you may be dealing with a troll:

1. Pretty much everything they say is inflammatory in some way.

2. They are very contradictory.

3. They put down your views.

4. They say things to sound smart.

5. When presented with evidence contrary to their own view, they either ignore it or do not accept it.

6. To paraphrase a post I saw on Facebook, reasoning with them is like trying to smell the color 9.

7. You try to cross a bridge and they make you pay a toll.

Trolls are something that most of us will have to deal with in some point in our life. The best way to smite a troll is the silent treatment. They absolutely can't stand being ignored. If ignored long enough, they lose interest and find some other person to pester.

You can't take what trolls say personally. It is their goal in life to push people's buttons, regardless of the circumstances.

Whilst trolls act smarter than you, other people just genuinely are smarter than you. I don't care how smart you are, go online and someone will make you feel stupid. Like physical geographical locations, various websites have their own culture. At some sites, people tend to lean towards cooperation, while others are just a place for people to lord their capabilities over you. It's not to say that geniuses making you look stupid is always a bad thing. It's happened to me plenty of times. It doesn't always feel the best, depending on how their information is presented, but I frequently learn from it. It's what I refer to as "the Xbox Live paradox."

Xbox Live is an online gaming service provided by Microsoft (my gamertag is Prevcha). It allows players to connect and compete against one another. My buddy Ryan and I frequently meet on Xbox Live and play each other *in Gears of War 3*. We've played tons of *Gears 3*. We have most of the achievements, medals and ribbons. We beat the game on insane difficulty. We competed against one another so frequently that the controls became like second nature. We were hands-down awesome at this game, or at least that's what the evidence suggested. Instead of just fighting each other, one day, we decided to compete against other players from around the world. When we played our first round, we thought there was some kind of weird technical glitch. I mean, we died so fast, we thought maybe the controls weren't working right. That had to be it, right? As it turns out, despite all of our hard work and achievements, we just are not that good at *Gears of War 3*. In fact, we are so lackluster that people we have played with previously will immediately quit if they see that we are on their team. Seems a bit harsh for a game, but let's call a spade a spade here. Being beat so thoroughly wasn't always fun, but I did learn a lot from it. I learned better movement and weapon strategies. I even learned some interesting and creative curse words. I took advantage of what those more skilled than myself taught me and I recommend that you do the same.

I have an internal need to try and be what our society considers a high achiever. I certainly don't think I am better than anyone else, but I do have accomplishments that I would think some people would consider at least mildly impressive. Those accomplishments, at least for me, have been hard work. When I hear about the 14 year old who created an app that just sold for millions of dollars, or the 20 year old that is still in college, but started an amazing dotcom in their spare time, it makes me a little crazy with jealousy.

The law of large numbers suggests that those types of things are bound to happen, but it still makes me feel like a big fat loser when I hear them. It doesn't help that those types of stories spread like wild fire considering how networked we are and the internet is rife with them.

In all likelihood, I will never have the aforementioned type of astronomical success, but truth-be-told, neither will most of us. It's so easy to compare yourself to the latest dotcom billionaire or the supermodel on the cover of vogue, but in many cases, it's like comparing apples to oranges. All of us come from vastly different circumstances which makes it difficult to compare your lot in life to someone else's. I've always liked the saying "you need to compare you to you." In other words, gauge where you are today and then periodically take some time to review. Are you considerably fatter than you were last year? Time to start eating better. Do you have more money in your account than you did this time last year? Congrats! Keep up the hard work!

I can't think of anything that I am the best at. I'm not sure I know anyone who is the best at something. I guess that's not entirely true, my other buddy, Colin, might be the best professional weight lifter in his weight class in the world, but that's a topic for another book. There was something, however that I was one of the best at.

Several years ago my wife introduced me to a television show call *Stargate SG-1*. It was a science fiction show that was based off of the *Stargate* movie. For those of you who are curious, a stargate is a wormhole connecting two points in the universe. She and her family used to watch the show together and since I like science fiction, she thought I might like it. She was wrong; initially anyway. The show was dreadful. The only saving grace of the first episode was the attractive nude lady about to be implanted with a worm like alien. That part I liked very much. The nude part, not the lady getting implanted, just to be clear. Although if the implanting part was of interest to me, I bet I could find a community on the internet to support me! I stuck with the show and by the time we finished watching season 3, I was hooked. Once I had a better handle on the characters and their motivations, it made it easier to relate to the story. Not to mention, the show just got considerably better overall. I was officially a *Stargate SG-1* fan.

Fast forward a few years and I came to find out that *Stargate Resistance*, a third-person, multiplayer shooter video game based on the show is in development. Being a fan, I followed the game's progress. It didn't closely follow any sort of official canon storyline, but the character classes were loosely based on the show and it looked like it could be fun.

When the game released, I picked up a copy and gave it shot. My sentiments for the game were similar to those of my first time watching *Stargate*; not very good. I think my impressions were largely due to a lack of understanding. I tried to configure a controller to work with the game and that made things confusing. I also died.....a lot. Like, so much so that I actually started laughing because it was just so ridiculous. After an afternoon of what can only be described as cruel and unusual punishment, I quit the game vowing to never return.

Approximately 10 days later, I sat down at the computer and I saw the *Stargate Resistance* icon just staring at me on my desktop. I was still healing from our last encounter, but something inside of me really wanted to click that thing. I have no idea what or where that feeling came from. I genuinely did not like the game, but for some reason, I launched it anyway. The game loaded up and I opted to be the Ashrak character; an evil alien assassin that could go invisible and shank unaware earthlings from the rear. My alien cohort and I stormed Stargate Command in order to thwart the humans' aspirations of exploring the universe and discovering technology that could defend them against my race's inevitable invasion. My character was about to make these bitches her slave.

Things did not start off well. The controls were, for lack of a better word, floaty. I kind of felt like my character was moving all over the place. I died. Then I died again. Three, four maybe five times and then, eureka! I successfully snuck up on a human scientist healing her mostly dead companion and with one fell swoop, took her out. Granted, the turret she built a meter and half back and to the left quickly dispatched of me once my invisibility shield came down, but the ends justified the means. I was finally met with a partial victory and as is so often the case, success breeds success.

I started taking out multiple players in a row before dying. Then I was at a point where I almost didn't die. Eventually I switched from the Ashrak to the System Lord class and became an incredibly effective controller, both taking people out and healing my own team.

The System Lord class had an ability that pushed opponents away with a hand movement. It really was Stargate's version of Force Push. Generally speaking, it was used as a defensive maneuver to push your opponent back and regroup. In certain instances, it could be used offensively to great effect. One of the maps in the game had a giant hole located in a heavily trafficked area. If a player wanted to traverse the north central part of the map and many of them did, they had little choice but to walk into the general proximity of this bottomless pit of despair. Directly west of this death trap was some shadowy area and structures that one could potentially hide in if conditions were right. Massive firefights near the pit area were not uncommon. Our Jaffa Troopers would fire off rounds and be met with heavy resistance. One of my favorite things to do was wait for a squad of 2-3 human characters come out and lay down heavy fire on our troopers while I made a hard b-line due east and force pushed those hapless bastards into the death pit.

At this point my skill had developed enough that I was getting recognition from the community. One of the developers of the game even referred to me as the mighty Prevch. I certainly wasn't the best player, but I was definitely one of the best. Now, being the best at a game really isn't going to change the world, but I will admit, the compliments were nice. Even better though, were the insults.

I felt like I had gone as far as I could go with the evil alien race. Now it was time to proudly defend my home planet as a human scientist. The scientist class was a controversial one. Not only could she heal her own team, she was a pretty effective killer with her ability to build turrets. I was a little luke warm on the turrets. Sure, they were effective killing machines, but they felt a little cheap the way they were implemented. My favorite thing in the world to do as the scientist was jump off of a ledge into a massive group of unsuspecting evil aliens, spray poison gas and run like I stole something. It was hilarious to see the pandemonium ensue. Green gas filled the air and opponents scatted like roaches. I had been on the receiving end of that poison more times than I cared to count, so I was familiar with the absolute devastation that it wrought. It was a high risk, high reward maneuver. If your opponents were already partly damaged, you could easily take out multiple at a time. If they were at full health, the likelihood of you being swarmed with an onslaught of laser weapons and brain scramblers were nigh 100%.

I remember one particular match I was playing against a very talented Ashrak. I can't remember his gamertag, but I'm pretty sure it had Raven in it. It was like DarkRaven or something along those lines. This guy was killing people left and right. He knew how to sneak, he knew how to kill and he knew how to evade. This was a truly great player. Me, always being up for a good challenge, decided that I wanted to take this guy out. He wasn't getting the one-man-army achievement (15 kills in a row without dying) on my watch. He was already at like 12, so I needed to act quick. I knew my ambush poison attack wasn't go to work. No, this guy moved too fast and too frequently for those kinds of cheap parlor tricks. This was going to be a head-to-head clash of the titans. Directly running up and spraying wasn't going to work either. The only other weapon that I had at my disposal was a weak pistol. If I ran up and sprayed and then tried to finish the job with my pistol, I was almost certainly dead. Planting a turret wasn't an option either. This guy knew most of the good plant points and if a turret was in the area, he just simply would not reveal himself. I didn't want a cheap turret death. I wanted a battle that minstrels would sing songs about. I had to come up with a plan and I had to do it quick. In only 3 more kills this guy was walking away with the most difficult achievement in the game. What I did next was not my proudest moment, but as they say, all is fair in love and war.

The overall player community was relatively small, but there were new players coming in all the time. Teams were often compiled of players with skill levels that ran the gamut. I certainly prefer it that way. I find that my favorite gaming communities are those that are actively supported and participated in by a wide array of players. I noticed that my team had a few beginner players. I mean, theses cats were green. They would just go and strike up a conversation while remaining stationary next to the pit of despair. Hell, even I wanted to pit them. Not because I wanted to see them die, but pitting people was just such a thrill in and of itself. One of our newbies was playing a soldier character and was scouring the map for enemies. His movements were slow and clunky. I totally remember being in his position and if history was any indicator, this guy was going to be dead and soon. I knew DarkRaven would see this guy sauntering around the map because I used to do the exact same thing. It was like a shark smelling blood in the water. This dude was a marked man. Knowing that DarkRaven had found the weak and the lame in our herd, I decided to follow Mr. Newb. I'm guessing he was excited to have a healing teammate by his side. Considering how many times he had already died, he could use someone backing him up. Unbeknownst to him, I had no intention of offering any type of aid.

I followed behind newb at a distance of approximately 2-3 body lengths. I knew that was plenty of distance for DarkRaven to sneak in and take him down, but not so far that I would miss with the poison spray. Yes, I was using my teammate as a decoy. Unlike Mr. Newb, I traveled in a serpentine pattern. It was much more difficult to backstab someone if they were traversing both vertically and horizontally. We were on the Northwest side of the map when the inevitable happened. DarkRaven swiped the blade, immediately laying out Mr. Newb while at the same time decloaking to become visible. This was my chance. I sprayed my poison and it was a hit! DarkRaven seemed to be at full health because he immediately started retreating. As quickly as I could, I switched to my piddly little pea shooter and started firing off rounds. DarkRaven could move. He was all over the place. Hitting him was proving exceptionally difficult. I got a couple shots in, but he was zig-zagging south at an incredible clip. I knew he had to be close to death, but he was practically on the other end of the map and this was a huge area. It got to the point where firing at him seemed almost pointless. He was just so far away. I had one single bullet left and nothing to lose. Based off of his movement pattern, I could only assume he was going to move back hard right. From this distance, it was practically impossible to judge the trajectory. I decided I had to lead him a little more than normal since the bullet had so far to travel. Incredibly, I led him by about a step-and-a-half and this guy's face ran directly into that bullet. At 13 kills and 0 deaths, he went down hard. What followed was one of the greatest moments of my life. He freaked. He started screaming "I hate you, Prevch! I [expletive deleted] hate you! I will kill you and your whole [expletive deleted] family!"

I cannot even explain to you how hard I laughed. It was like getting recognition from a great player, but also finding it humorous how seriously this guy took the game. I rubbed it in a little bit. I replied something like "Aww hard cheese" or "That's the way the cookie crumbles" or something similar.

The moral of the story is, if you get good enough at something, you can lord your abilities over others just like they have done to you! You really shouldn't do that, but you should pass your knowledge onto others. I think it's important to remember where we came from. I didn't start out as a great *Stargate Resistance* player. I watched the good players and asked them questions to improve my capabilities. Most people don't start out great at anything. It takes hard work to develop one's skills and it's important to recognize that all of our accomplishments can generally be attributed to the knowledge of others and their willingness to help. (Or make us feel stupid with how great they are.)

Stargate Resistance being the obvious exception, most things I am just adequate at. I frequently try to take on new projects and am often left feeling less-than-stellar on my first attempt. By almost all accounts, my failure is a direct result of my own negligence which makes it that much more difficult to palette.

When something happens that makes me feel stupid or less accomplished, I tend to obsess about it. I hate feeling that way, but nothing has taught me more than my own failures and shortcomings. I'm learning to embrace them for what they are, the best teaching tool in the world and an incredible motivator.

Chapter 2 practical recommendations:

1. Get involved with a community of interest online

2. Compare yourself only to you and others like you

3. Embrace failure and people making you feel stupid. It will happen often.

4. Don't feed trolls!

CHAPTER 3: YOUR BRAND - PORTRAYING YOURSELF ONLINE

We all wear masks. I don't wear the same mask in front of my buddies that I do in front of my grandma. I'm still the same person at my core, but if I said and did the things in front of my grandma that I do in front of my pals, she'd be liable to drop dead of a heart attack. Admittedly, there are times when I perform poorly when I should be filtering myself, but by-and-large I operate well in most situations.

To participate in the analog world, most of us need to adhere to the social constructs we find ourselves in. I wouldn't show up in a Hawaiian shirt for a job interview, for example. My buddy, Becca went to a job interview and when the interviewer asked her to describe her background, she replied "Well, I'm a Cancer and that already tells you way more than you need to know." I wouldn't recommend that either. In Becca's defense, I should tell you that she had already decided that she didn't want the job once she started the interview because they were so rude to her. She's not just some crazy nut job. I mean, she is, but for other, more awesome reasons.

I was interviewing for a leadership position at an IT company and one of the questions was "How much would you expect to be paid to do this job?" I replied, "I don't know, how much do you got?" Again, perhaps not the best move, but I did get a rise out of the guy.

My parents and teachers did a fine job of teaching me appropriate behavior in face-to-face situations, but no one ever schooled me in online etiquette. Let's face it, it's the wild west out there. I'm often shocked at what some people will put up on their Facebook pages. They'll take party pictures of themselves smoking drugs, post the evidence on Facebook and then wonder why the police show up at their door. I tell you what, next time, just save the justice system some time and drop off a Polaroid of yourself hitting the bong at the police station, it'll be quicker for everyone involved.

Images are a powerful form of nonverbal communication. When we see someone, especially for the first time, we pass judgments and make assumptions. Even for the most open-minded people, humans can't help but relate something about a person to some experience they have previously had. Evolutionarily, this makes sense. We need to be ever alert to the potential of danger or the possibility of finding a mate in order to preserve our species.

Dave Chapelle did a bit about seeing women in the club who are provocatively dressed and trying to make a pass at them only to be met with the woman being appalled that he would think he could approach a lady in such a manner just because she is dressed a certain way. He admitted that it is absolutely true your manner of dress does not necessarily represent who you are as a person, but he also went on to explain just how incredibly confusing that is. He told the crowd to imagine that he, as a comedian, was walking down the street in a cop's uniform. The victim of a robbery ran up to him and pleaded for his help. "Please, help me! The bad guys are right over there! Arrest them!" He then responded "Whoa, whoa, whoa, hang on for just a minute here. You think just because I am dressed like this, I am an officer of the law." It was a great bit, but it was an ever better point. People who don't know you, like a dude in a bar or the victim of some random crime, will try to garner information about you from your appearance.

Judgment of your appearance is exacerbated online. It's certainly plausible that many of the people viewing your photos online, don't personally know you. They may just be friends of friends, but they may also be future employers. For those of us who choose to participate online, we need to accept that we are public figures. Sure, there are settings on social media sites that allow us to filter who sees our information, but what if a friend downloads a picture and shares it? What if your account gets hacked? I know several people who have had their social media accounts hijacked. I always recommend to people to operate under the assumption that anything they say or do on a data network is public.

The consequences of that can potentially be astronomical. The sexy picture you snapped of yourself that was meant for your significant other's eyes only, just went viral and there is a lot of judgment coming down on your location.

Let's do a fun exercise. I'm going to put some pictures of myself below and develop a first impression of what you think I might be like. What are my values? Am I a nice person? Am I a self-centered jerk? Whatever you think of, just let it rip. Bear in mind, that this is a somewhat skewed exercise. For those of you who know me, you already have a pretty good idea of how you feel about me. For those who don't, you have already read this far in my book, so you might have already formed some opinions. Even so, for the sake of experimentation, let's give it a shot. After you're done checking out the pictures, we can compare answers.

Picture #1 - I'm on the right

My thoughts - If I was to see this picture having no other context, I would guess that these are low achieving kids trying to look ghetto. I would assume that their priorities are not well organized. I would likely guess that they abuse some type of substance.

Your thoughts -

The truth - Me and my hetero life mate Chris, two relatively well behaved, average kids, went to the thrift shop and found clothes we could wear to school in an attempt to emulate an over-the-top gangsta' look. This was pretty common practice at my school circa 2000. The black pants I had on were like a weird mixture of shiny denim and pleather. If you've ever wanted to simulate what it might be like to wear a hot greenhouse from the waist down, I recommend tightly woven, shiny denim pleather pants.

Picture #2

My thoughts - This one is a little tougher. I mean, clearly it's a man in a shiny coat paired with bedazzled purple bikini briefs over his jeans, but there are not a lot of context clues. He's holding his finger to his lips and has a somewhat "come hither" expression, so I might guess that it's a Halloween costume that I don't understand. I might also guess that he has just had a few too many drinks. I might possibly suspect that he is homosexual.

Your thoughts -

The truth – No, it wasn't Halloween and I did indeed have my fair share of the delicious ambrosia known as *Beer 30*. This picture was taken in the parking lot of a professional wrestling show. My buddies and I used to occasionally attend the shows of a local wrestling federation. It was pretty goofy, as all professional wrestling is, but it was still a great time.

One of the wrestler's names was Trevor. The first time I saw him compete, he wore the tiniest little purple trunks you ever saw in your life. He also did some very rhythmic disco tech dance moves. I felt like it took a lot of courage to get in front of a crowd and dance in such a skimpy outfit, (shout out to the strippers of the world) so the next time we went to a show, I decided to make my own tiny, little purple trunks with a sparkly heart and Trevor written on the butt.

As luck would have it, Trevor was there that night. As he gyrated down the aisle to ringside, I jumped up proudly displaying his name upon my rump and we disco'd all the way to the ring. I even got a hug.

After the show, some of the wrestlers, my buddies and I hit up the bar. Despite being straight, I was met with some homophobia. I was really offended to hear one guy say "I didn't know they let fairies in here." Granted, having just retold the story, I guess I can somewhat understand their confusion, but that really doesn't give them the right to be rude. What if I was gay? Would it really make a difference to who I am as a person? Should I not have the same right as a straight person to go to a bar and enjoy spending time with my friends? I didn't know wearing purple trunks automatically made me gay. Apparently, all gay people dress and act a certain way.

I've always had a hard time stomaching hate rooted in ignorance. Morgan Freeman was quoted as saying "I hate the word homophobia. It's not a phobia. You are not scared. You are an asshole." Here, here, Morgan Freeman. Here, here.

Picture #3 - I'm on the left

My thoughts - I think this picture would leave me to believe this is a young, straight man having a great time dancing with an attractive young woman. It looks like the young lady might have a tattoo on her left arm, so maybe she is a bit of a party animal. I would also guess that the young man either loves dancing, music or both. I mean, no one smiles that big while they are having a bad time. I would also probably guess that the two of them might be in a romantic relationship.

Your thoughts -

The truth – This was taken at my buddy Jocelyn's 21st birthday party. We were indeed having a great time and I do indeed enjoy music and dancing. The alleged tattoo on her left arm was actually magic marker that read "I'm 21 [expletive deleted]!" I might take issue with the "attractive young woman" part of my impression. Don't get me wrong, Jocelyn is a very attractive woman, but at her 21st birthday party, she was a wreck. Lastly, despite our great love for each other's company, Jocelyn and I were not, nor have we ever been in a romantic relationship. She did, however, end up in my bed that night. Not for any romantic reason, she just literally slept there. I guess I should also mention that at the time this picture was taken, we were roommates.

Picture #4 - I'm in the middle

My thoughts - I would guess this picture is of a happy, straight, newlywed couple listening to a groomsman give a speech. The couple seems to be average, middle class Americans.

Your thoughts -

The truth – This one is relatively easy. The picture is pretty much what it looks like. The most interesting thing about this picture is my reaction to what you don't hear. Notice that I am looking down with my hands over my face, laughing hysterically, but then also embarrassingly wondering what the people in the audience are thinking about what my cousin Derek is saying. I literally could not bear to look the crowd in the eye.

Like any good best man speech, he made the whole audience question my morals and sexual identity. Bear in mind, that there are several people here that I hardly even know. I can't remember the speech verbatim, but I have recreated what I remember for your reading pleasure:

I'm Derek, Ethan's cousin.

When I first heard that Ethan was marrying Natalie, I felt anger, hatred.....betrayal and then someone told me he wasn't marrying my sister, he was marrying his girlfriend and I was like oh that's cool.

Ethan had no idea that he was going to get a lightsaber during the grand march so, all of that you just saw, whatever that was, was all locked and loaded and the second nerdiest thing I have ever seen.

crowd: What was the first?

The first was a 40 year old man walked into my shop with a Marvin the Martian hat, shirt and fanny pack on and I was just like you have to leave before I beat you up.

Growing up I always looked up to Ethan especially with video games. I remember trying to beat this surfing part in *BattleToads* where you go over this ledge thing and I would die in the same spot like 160 times and then I would go downstairs to get some food and come back and he would have already beaten it and I was like that's amazing, I will follow you anywhere, so yeah, you're my hero.

Like you I had my doubts about Ethan. I mean, he accepted an invitation to a Prince concert from a man in leather pants....granted that man was me, but accepting the invitation was still pretty gay.

Unfortunately, that's all I remember and it's not

recorded, but things continued to go downhill from there. I would just like to clarify that Derek is not anti-gay in any way, he was just trying to stir the pot.

Picture #5

My thoughts - It looks like the groom from the previous picture snuck out a side door. From the look on his face, it seems like he either did something mischievous or his is seeking out some trouble to get in to.

Your thoughts -

The truth – I did go out the side door and I did have a mischievous look on my face, but I was just checking on routine wedding stuff.

Picture #6 - I'm in the middle

My thoughts - It looks like the groom found the trouble he was looking for! He wants one more wild soiree with a group of pretty ladies before he is tied down forever!

Your thoughts -

The truth – A great picture with the beautiful bridesmaids. This was obviously a bit of a silly example, but it's interesting to note that the order of a group of pictures, be they related or otherwise, could tell a story all their own.

Picture #7

My thoughts - I would guess one of two things from this picture. Either one, this is a grown man who just enjoys wearing a cape and a mask or two it's some kind of practical joke. The background would suggest that he is at some type of work environment and he is dressed in pretty standard clothes, so I'm guessing he is an average, middle class guy. He is clearly willing to wear a costume at work, so he must not take himself too seriously.

Your thoughts -

The truth – The truth happens to be an amalgamation of my initial impressions. I am a middle class working man who does not take himself too seriously and I also enjoy wearing capes and masks, but this particular getup was worn because I won a prize. Work allows us to donate part of our paychecks to student scholarships. One of the benefits of doing so, other than the obvious financial assistance that we provide to our students, is that we are periodically entered into drawings for prizes. I was lucky enough to win a prize and get my picture taken. We had the option to have our picture taken in a superhero costume and naturally I chose to do so.

Picture #8 - I'm on the left

My thoughts - My impression of picture #8 is one of a young couple enjoying themselves at what seems to be an outdoor party. It looks like they are enjoying some adult beverages, but the dude is holding an entire pitcher and his date is not drinking beer. I think this guy might have a problem.

Your thoughts -

The truth – Natalie and I were celebrating with friends and family in our hometown of Monroe, WI at the Cheese Days Festival. I highly recommend checking out Cheese Days if you've never gone, it can be a great time. Indeed, I am holding an entire pitcher of beer, but what the picture doesn't explain is that I was serving a group of several people around us.

Picture #9

My thoughts - Why is the guy dressed like George Michael? I wonder if he is gay.

Your thoughts -

The truth – I love George Michael, so I thought it would be fun to try and semi-impersonate his look from the *Faith* album. (Amazing album by the way.) As of this writing, this is my Facebook profile pic. Yeah, I keep it classy like that.

I hope you found that to be a fun an informative exercise. You'll notice in the "My Thoughts" portions that I frequently refer to the potential socioeconomic status and sexuality of the subjects. I think it's natural for humans to automatically ask those questions when they first see/meet people. It's like we have this constant need to compare.

Keeping that in mind, it's important to remember that when we display ourselves online, we create a certain brand/image that we portray to others. What do you want your brand to be? Do you think your brand is going to change over time? If so, what decisions do you need to make today in order to make that a smoother transition in the future?

Most of the above pictures are relatively harmless. I would feel comfortable using most of them on a social media site like Facebook, but there are a few that might best be suited for my own, offline picture collection. Whether you are posting pictures, video, or just sharing a text update, be aware of not only the message you want to send, but how the message could potentially be perceived and misconstrued by others. Further, regardless of your security settings, always assume that your online media is not private.

None of the above pictures would be appropriate for a professional social media site such as LinkedIn because none of the above photos are resume appropriate. Ok, maybe if I wanted to be a George Michael impersonator, one of the pictures could go on a LinkedIn profile page.

A picture is worth a thousand words, but what about words themselves? A lot of our interaction online is written, so it's important to remember a few rules.

Even if you are not a great writer, it's important to use some basic punctuation. The message "Let's eat Mom" and "Let's eat, Mom" are two totally different messages thanks to one tiny little comma. I also frequently see people write in huge run-on sentences. It's incredibly difficult to make sense of a sentence that has 17 subjects and not one complete thought.

Typing in all capital letters represents shouting. Apparently, if you were to translate the text "I'M A CALM, WELL ADJUSTED INDIVIDUAL IN FULL CONTROL OF MY EMOTIONS AND FACULTIES" from written form to spoken word, you would be screaming the phrase at the top of your lungs. I've seen several posts from people that don't understand the all-caps rule and they end up offending people who are aware of it.

Tread carefully when communicating the tone of your message. In audible communication, it's easy to express feelings through the tone of your voice. Naturally, that luxury is completely lost when writing. You could make an innocent, sarcastic joke and end up looking like a real jerk if your message is not received in the spirit in which it was intended. I'm not sure there is any one-size-fits-all solution to this problem, but one popular method I have seen online is to actually label your message's tone to eliminate any confusion. For example, if I was to say *Safe and Sound* was the best song ever, some people might believe I was being genuine and that is just not acceptable. If I wanted to be absolutely sure that people understood the tone of my message, I could preface it like so: [sarcasm] *Safe and Sound* is the best song ever. [/sarcasm] The [/sarcasm] part means that I am closing the sarcasm tag so, presumably, what I say next should not be sarcastic. [truth]*Purple Rain* is the best song ever![/truth]

The / closing idea comes from hyper text markup language, one of the computer languages people use to develop web pages.

The opening and closing tone tags can be used just as easily for a number of different tonal expressions. [excited][/excited], [angry][/angry], [joyful][/joyful], etc.

A telephone tough guy is someone who acts tougher or is more aggressive on the phone than they ever would be in real life. Some online users suffer from a similar phenomenon. Apparently, if you say something awful while covered in the anonymity that the internet provides, that makes it ok. I guess we could refer to them as internet tough guys, but the behavior I'm referring to goes well beyond just acting tough and certainly isn't exclusive to males. In fact, I'm not sure anyone is meaner to each other online than women. Since internet tough guy doesn't really cover it, I'm going to refer to this group of offenders as "Net Nasties."

Net Nasties are similar to trolls in a lot of ways and I think there is some crossover, but there is one main difference. Generally speaking, trolls are often just trying to get a rise out of the community they are engaging in. Net Nasties are being genuinely mean. I think cyber bullies would fall under this category. Very few people would walk up to someone's face and call them a fat, ugly, bleepety bleep, yet they harbor no hesitation to text or email it. The golden rule seems to be a wonderful guide for communication of all forms. For those unaware, the golden rule states "Treat others how you want to be treated." We start finding holes in the golden rule in the S&M community, but by-and-large, it's a safe rule of thumb.

If you find that you're too big of a blowhard to be a decent human being in your online interactions, I challenge you to take responsibility for them. If you plan on calling someone a fat, ugly, bleepety bleep online, stop yourself and confront them face-to-face. If you're willing to do so, it's quite likely that this is something that you need to get off your chest. Of course, be prepared to handle the potential consequences and fallout from your actions.

I understand that some things are incredibly difficult to say face-to-face. There have been times in my life that I have preferred receiving a written communication over a spoken one. It allowed me to process and reflect on the message prior to giving a response. That being said, none of those profound messages were off-the-cuff insults. I've never sat down and deeply reflected on someone calling me a fat, ugly, bleepety bleep. Tact is not strictly an analog social convention.

Whether portraying yourself online or off, just remember that there are no second, first impressions.

Chapter 3 practical recommendations:

1. Actively think about how you want to portray yourself online. What does your brand look like? Do you see it changing in the future?

2. Review your online media and communications. Update and modify as necessary.

3. Practice reviewing the punctuation of your written messages. Could your message be misinterpreted due to improper punctuation?

4. Practice reviewing the tone of your written messages. Could your message be misinterpreted due to an unintended tone?

5. Take a writing course to make punctuating and communicating tone easier!

6. Play the first impression picture game with your friends and family using your own pictures!

7. Follow the golden rule in your communications.

CHAPTER 4: YOUR PARTICIPATION AND ITS VALUE - SHARING YOUR GIFTS AND FILTERING CRITICISM

Good online citizenship requires keeping an open mind by reevaluating biases and not being afraid to fail. It also requires that you present an image appropriate to your goals and a certain level of civility, but above all, it demands your participation.

The internet is the great equalizer. 20 years ago I would have never dreamed of writing a book on a topic that I was passionate about and self publishing it on Amazon. Granted, 20 years ago I was 10 years old, the book probably would have been about Swiss Cake Rolls and Amazon didn't exist, but hopefully you get my point. The landscape has changed. The independent author/musician/entertainer still does not have all of the advantages that the big boys have, but at least now they have an opportunity.

Even if the Internet did not have the somewhat equalizing effect that it has, it's nothing without you. The internet is just an infrastructure. It's just a bunch of computers hooked together that can communicate. Not that I'm discounting the unbelievable engineering behind network communication, it is truly awe inspiring, but without creator's websites, songs, poems, photography, research, stories, editorials, etc. it's nothing but an empty highway.

Back in high school, we had an annual talent shown known as the revue. Any student could put an act together and audition for a time slot. I've never really thought of myself as having any sort of outstanding talent, but I did want to participate. Being a Michael Jackson fan and having the ability to carry a tune, I decided I was going to do a MJ themed act.

Choosing the act was only the first step. If I wanted to win one of those time slots, I was going to have to deliver. My first thoughts were on image. I needed to look flashy. I wanted to be reminiscent of MJ, but I didn't want to be an absolute carbon copy. I started scouring every closet in the house. I found some black dress pants and a pair of leather dress shoes that were slippery on the bottom (essential for a convincing moonwalk) and they had a gold buckle on the top. Perfect. Some more searching led to the discovery of a dingy, old black t-shirt. The dinginess was not a factor since the lights would be low during the performance. Better yet, no one would care if I customized an old t-shirt with a pair of scissors. I was getting close. I had a pair of white socks that would pair well with the black pants and shoes and I had previously purchased a fedora hat from the thrift store for my role as Sky Masterson in *Guys and Dolls*, but something was still missing.

I really wanted to wear a sparkly white glove, but it's not like you could just go to Wal-Mart and pick one up. My treasure hunt led me to the entry closet. A little organizational Feng Shui led to the discovery of a plastic bag full of winter items. Amongst them was a pair of white gloves. You know, the cheap, knit kind that don't provide any protection from the elements. This would work perfect, but I still needed to find some way to make them sparkle.

To my knowledge, no one in my family owned a Bedazzler at the time. I'm sure we owned one in the 80's and it was probably stored right next to our Lite Brite and Teddy Ruxpin, but that was of no help at this particular moment. We had two side attic rooms in the upstairs of our bungalow that were smattered with stuff. If I was going to find sparkles, I was going to find them there.

Traversing the first attic room was like drudging through a tightly packed garage sale with attention deficit disorder. There was no common theme to the items. From Mt. Books to the Great Shoe Ravine, the topography was a cornucopia of offerings. Worse yet, the room was completely off the grid as far as HVAC was concerned. If it was a sunny, 70 degree day outside, it was an overcast, 180 degrees in the attic. I remained hopeful.

I felt like a secret agent performing a high stakes heist. Sweat was rolling down my brow as I carefully tiptoed around the security obstacles trying to keep me from my glittery prize. Of course, there was no guarantee that I was going to find any sort of decorative material in here at all. I was just as likely to die of heat stroke as I was to find what I needed. I lifted, I twisted and I begrudgingly swam through the pool of belongings and after what felt like an eternity of searching, I found nothing. Dripping with sweat and laden with disappointment, I left.

The experience I had in the first attic room was enough to make me want to give up. I was so hot and uncomfortable. I just wanted to have a bowl of ice cream and take a shower. I was actually contemplating taking the half gallon of cookies 'n' cream in the shower with me; truly, a new low in terms of consumption. As heavy as the feelings of defeat were weighing upon me, I decided I had to look in attic room number two.

The second attic room was directly across the hall from the first. I rarely opened this door, but I knew that if I saw the same landscape that I did in the first room, part of my soul was going to die. I placed my hand on the door knob and I remember letting out a sigh. As I turned the knob, the door popped open a bit and a rush of what felt like magma charged air came pouring out. This was going to be a disaster. I swung the door open as wide as I could then quickly fanned it back and forth like I was going to magically cool down this room that had been baking for hours. I took a step in, turned on the light and immediately to my left was a bag of crafting materials. In the bag of crafting materials was three quarters of a roll of sequin laced fabric. The drama of opening the door literally took longer than finding the material. I didn't know whether to laugh or cry, so I did both and went to the freezer to get the ice cream.

My Mom had an orange Tupperware full of sewing materials in the downstairs bathroom hall closet, so I grabbed a needle and thread and made off back upstairs to my room to begin construction. I was already tired by the time work on the glove began. Gathering the required materials demanded a hearty amount of inter-home travel. The exhaustion was exacerbated from the mild heat stroke I was experiencing. I needed to refocus. The question at hand (pun intended) was how does one appropriately cover a cheap winter glove in sequins. I didn't know the answer to that question then and I don't know now. All I knew was that the glove needed to sparkle.

I unrolled the sequin fabric and just started lopping off sections. Sequin particles were flailing about as I tried to cut reasonably shaped pieces to cover the exposed white spots. For such a small article of clothing, I used enough thread for the patch job to withstand hurricane force winds. I don't know how many different stitching techniques there are, but I'm confident that shades of all of them were poorly represented in the development of this stage prop.

I was amazed at how long this project took. Every time I felt like I was making significant progress, I ran into a problem like a sewed shut finger hole or just a sewed finger. By the time the glove was adequately covered, it reminded me of a sparkly pine bush that hadn't been pruned for a few seasons. There was gobs of gangly thread shooting off in every direction. I wanted to just trim the thread down, but I had no clue what I was doing. As far as I knew, those stray threads were all that was holding this train wreck together. Cutting one of those things could compromise the structural integrity of the whole project, but I couldn't just leave them there. It was like I was on the bomb squad and it was my job to defuse an active threat. Should I cut the red wire or the blue wire? Maybe I should cut the yellow wire. Like any reasonable person, I grabbed a bunch of stray threads, closed my eyes and cut them all. To my surprise, the thing stayed together. A couple of my sequin strips moved around a little bit, but everything was intact. I mowed the rest of the glove and moved on to the next project.

The socks were not nearly as much of a challenge. All I had to do was wrap the material around the perimeter and sew it into place. This was one of the less visible parts of the project, so presentability was more of an afterthought.

I tried the outfit on and while I was happy with the gloves and the socks, neck to knickers I was looking pretty Plain-Jane. I looked like the goth version of an MJ impersonator. The decision had been made, my shirt needed to be flashier.

After the experience I had just had with the gloves and the socks, I absolutely loathed the idea of putting sequins all over the entirety of the shirt. I decided that I was going to lay out a simple sparkly pattern and call it a day. I cut a few strips of material and randomly laid out a pattern. It was a fairly good sized shape that covered a large portion of the front of the shirt. The thought of sewing that whole thing was repugnant. Being the shortcut artist that I was, I went to my dresser and opened the bottom drawer. The bottom drawer was known as the drawer of the miscellaneous. Amongst the scattering of batteries, shoestrings and duct tape was exactly what I needed, a stapler. I methodically stapled the pattern onto the shirt making sure that the pointy spikes that peaked through to the inside were flattened so as not to disturb some of my more sensitive parts. Minutes later, I was ready to try on the outfit again.

I got dressed and upon standing in front of my full length mirror, I was met with the image of what resembled a cheap entertainer. Great Scott! I was ready to put on a show.

Closer inspection of the pattern revealed that it resembled a backwards number four. It was like the *Fantastic Four* got a shiny new member, Dr. Liberace. Despite Dr. Liberace's advanced degree, he forgot to not adhere his insignia upon his chest while looking in the mirror. For the record, in the off chance that Marvel decides to adopt Dr. Liberace as a character, I want his super power to be mesmerizing jazz hands.

This costume looked exactly how you would expect. Up close, it looked like an unfortunate home-ec debacle, but from a distance, in a dimly lit room, it looked pretty awesome.

Now that I had the threads, I needed an act. *Billie Jean* seemed like the most natural choice, but I always partial to the song *Dirty Diana*. I decided to mix the two. I would start off with a short dance number to *Billie Jean* and then sing *Dirty Diana*.

My full length mirror served as my practice stage. This was not ideal. It was certainly tall enough to accommodate my stature, but one side step took me completely out of frame. It got to the point where I leaned the mirror back horizontally along the wall just so I could get a good look at my footwork. I was nervous. If I was going to do this, I had to do it right.

My dance routine had all the fixings of a classic MJ ditty. I started off with a staccato swipe across my fedora, moved into the kicked, spun and hit a moonwalk. From there, I moved directly into part of his routine from Motown 25, pelvic pumps and all. The dance was ready.

I'm a fairly confident singer, but the vocal on *Dirty Diana* is bananas. I knew I would be out of breath after the dance routine and that song required oxygen reserves. I probably practiced singing it 100 times and 98 of those times something went awry. A little turning blue from lack of oxygen here, a pubescent screech there, it was all fair game. Tryouts were right around the corner and the wrinkles just were not ironed out.

When I arrived for my tryout, my stomach felt like it was doing the Macarena. I walked into a room full of school administrators and fellow students. The judging panel was comprised of some faculty and administrators as well as a few students. Several of the young ladies on the panel were pretty foxy. The stakes just got a lot higher. Now, my upcoming performance would not only determine if I got to participate in the revue, it was also going to determine if I was going to go to prom. That stomach Macarena just upgraded to the Jitter Bug.

The tryout venue was abysmal. I was sandwiched between a piano, some cardboard boxes, a microphone, some crackling speakers and a tangled anaconda of audio cable. How I was going to dance amongst this wreckage remained to be seen. As previously mentioned, my stage wear really looked best under dim light. This particular setting was doused in bright, unforgiving florescent tubes. The panel had to notice that this outfit was cobbled together from spare parts.

I distinctly remember some subdued smiles as I approached the mic. These were not smiles of adoration, they were smiles of hilarity. Bear in mind that this was 2002. Michael Jackson was not exactly in favor amongst my peers; nor were sequins. This was a bold move. This was either going to end in a glowing success or a tsunami of ridicule.

The music started and like I had done 100 times before, I swiped my hand across my fedora, side kicked my leg in the air, nailed a spin and hit the moonwalk. Snafu number one occurred when I moonwalked directly into the audio cable anaconda. I had already gone a few steps back, so the judges got a good sense of my ability to do the move. I stopped in Anaconda's territory and filled the dead air with a couple of shoulder pops. It was now time to move into the *Billie Jean* Motown 25 dance part of the act. Snafu number two occurred when I turned to the side, slightly bent my knees, pointed my index finger on my right hand toward the ground, placed my left hand on my lower abdomen and started popping my pelvis to the beat. The trouble was, I was popping on the 1 and the 3 and not where I should have been, on the 2 and the 4. This is a common white guy problem. The reaction from the judges seemed positive, so I maintained my mistimed thrusts.

I had gotten through the dancing portion of the act relatively unscathed. My biggest obstacle now was trying to get sound to come out of my mouth during the singing portion. Between the aerobic stress of the dance and the gut wrenching nerves I was experiencing, a good breath was a rare commodity.

The room I was performing in was not very large. Honestly, they could have set a mic up just for show and heard me perfectly fine, but no, the mic was paired with speakers that were manufactured approximately the same time as the steam engine and they were barbarically loud. I'm not sure who set the levels on those things, but the minute the first lyric came out of my mouth, I had to pull myself back. Parts of *Dirty Diana* require a pretty large dynamic range. Snafu number three occurred when I realized that I would be responsible for the partial hearing loss of the judging panel during the loud parts of the song. I did my best to keep the mic as far away from me as possible during the more dynamic parts of the song, but I just was not blessed with long enough arms. I hit those notes and the speakers sounded like they were bleeding. Some of the judges got a somewhat uncomfortable looks on their face, but it seemed like I was not the first person they had experienced this problem with. Apparently, they decided to leave the speakers at mind altering levels just to make it fair for everyone.

At one point in Michael Jackson's *Dirty Diana* video, he hits a spin move, drops to his knees, tears his shirt open and suggestively thrusts his hips while singing Diana's name. I felt it was necessary to honor the source material, but I certainly wasn't willing to waste the perfectly good staple job that I had performed on my shirt, so the knee drop hip thrust was in and the shirt tear was out.

Snafu number four occurred when it was time to perform that climatic maneuver. I theatrically twirled the mic, hit the spin and dropped to the floor with the force of an F5 tornado. Early findings on the knee to floor impact suggested a dislocated right patella. Being the consummate amateur professional that I was, I continued the routine without hesitation. While writhing my hips with the conviction of a Chippendale dancer and crying out Diana's name, a quick survey of the judge's panel revealed some interesting reactions. Based solely on facial expression and body language, I determined that some of the faculty members were feeling my rock 'n' roll vibe. The student judges were a mixed bag of embarrassment and laughter and the principle was totally and utterly appalled.

As luck would have it, my patella was not detached and I was able to get back into an appropriate bipedal position. As the audition came to a close, the panel, with the exception of the principle of course, erupted in cheers. Weeks of work and stress had paid off in a successful audition. I went on to perform my act, sans Chippendale hip thrust, at the revue on two separate nights to a roaring and receptive crowd. It was a great memory and one I will never forget.

Coincidentally, all that practice paid off later in my life. My father-in-law's stipulation to marrying his daughter was that I had to dance like MJ at the wedding. I didn't put a routine together or anything like that, I just did a little improv to *Billie Jean*. The resulting chaos may be viewed here: http://www.youtube.com/watch?v=_-azUAsIxDk

So, what's my point? The Revue is just like the internet. It's an avenue that allows creators the ability to share their work. As you we all know, putting yourself out there can be an incredibly jarring experience. I could have just as easily fell flat on my face during the audition and made a total fool of myself, but had I not tried, I would have never been able to create such an awesome memory. Without its performers, the Revue does not exist.

Like the Revue, the Internet needs our content. Its lifeblood is our creativity and we all have something to offer. You don't have to be an expert. Just find something you are interested in and participate. Do you like trying to solve computer problems? Great! Find a computer forum and put in your two cents worth. Do you want to be an electrical engineer? Awesome! Build an electrically powered model car and share your work on YouTube. Are you a photographer? Fantastic! Build a website to share your portfolio.

Since you're a photographer, I need to ask you a question. Why is it that when a group of girls get together for a photo, particularly in a bar, club or wedding, they all get into a funny half squat position? It's like suddenly the force of gravity doubles and they simultaneously partly collapse. Are they under the impression that they are running the risk of getting part of their head cut off in the photograph? The majority of girl-group-squat-shots I have seen have had ample head room for proper posture. It's a curious phenomenon. I've talked to a lot of dudes and not once has one said "You know what I wish….."

I heard a female comedian once claim that 90% of what women do is to get a potential partner's attention. I'm certain that's not true, but for the sake of argument, let's assume that's the case. If indeed one was trying to look attractive, I would take the polar opposite approach to the semi-crouched position. I don't know about you, but the further I squat, the more liable my belly skin is to form rolls. I actually recommend that from now on, all potential squat shots become extended reach pictures. It makes sense. By standing on your tiptoes and jettisoning your arms straight up in the air, you give the illusion that you are taller than you really are, you show off your body and you'll never look skinnier than when you're at full extension, but I digress.

Keep in mind that your questions are equally as important as your contributions. In addition to expanding your own horizons, your queries may lead others to discover new passions and possibilities.

Taking that idea a step further, it's you responsibility to share your findings. How many times have you gained knowledge from some kind of resource or experiment and just stowed it away in your brain? I'm not suggesting you plagiarize someone's work, but the more information we share, the greater our knowledge base grows lifting society as a whole.

For example, a year or so ago, I was working with some hard drive backup software that was not cooperating. I read the documentation, asked for help in the forums and did several of my own experiments all to avail. Eventually, I came up with a harebrained workaround to get it operational. Needless to say, I don't use that software anymore, but once I figured out the issue, I went back to the manufacturer's forum and explained my methodology. Was it a little extra work? Sure, but imagine the amount of time it may have saved hundreds of other users.

Don't operate under the assumption that if you know it, surely everyone else does. Help improve our community by sharing your knowledge and insights.

Your job as a citizen in this brave new world is to participate. Get Started.

Here are some ideas for places that you can participate:

Social Media Sites such as Facebook and Google Plus

Video Communities like YouTube

Photography communities like Instagram

Marketplace communities like Ebay and Amazon

Independent music communities like CD Baby

Forums like Tom's Hardware

Video game communities like GameSpot

Interest sharing communities like Pinterest

Website communities like Wix

Independent contractor communities like Fiverr

And many, many others

So, you've taken my words to heart and you decide that you are going to utilize your undying passion for tap dancing and create a video. You know that you have never taken a tap dancing class in your life and the only black shoes you have are that old pair of Reebok Pumps with the orange basketball on the tongue, but I was so convincing in my plea for your creativity that you decide to move forward. What could possibly go wrong?

You grab your fancy suit, top hat, white gloves, cane and Reebok Pumps and start tapping out a few numbers. A solid five minutes of practice boosts your confidence enough that you decide it's time to go public. Of course, you've sweated out your suit at this point, but you don't have time to change, so you fire up your video camera and let it rip.

You're confident that your tap rendition of Beyonce's *Single Ladies* is going to be a YouTube sensation. You immediately upload the video and eagerly await the adoration of your fans.

The first few comments that roll in are pretty non-specific. There are several haha's and a sprinkling of OMG's, but nothing really concrete one way or the other. You decide to take a break and check in on things later.

After a much needed shower and a short nap, you decide to check back on your video for some additional feedback. Users have become significantly more specific with their feelings since you lest reviewed them. Phrases such as "sweaty, disabled penguin" and "poorly coordinated cow" became popular amongst the community.

It's at this point that you start cursing my name. What went wrong? You followed my advice to a T!

In response to your question, I would say nothing went wrong. You had an idea, you executed it and you shared it. No idea is ever met with universal praise. There are people out there who don't like Oreos. (if you call those people.) Sometimes when you share art, research, ideas, plans, etc. they end up not being validated in the way in which you intended. Sometimes your ideas are completely panned and sometimes they are validated in other ways.

You leave your video up because your Mom enjoys showing her friends, but you forget about it because you don't want to relive the humiliation of the comments other users left. A week later, you are bored and decide to check out your video once more. To your surprise, the video has over a million views! The sweaty, disabled penguin dance has gone viral! You notice that they are videos of people in dance clubs doing your dance to Beyonce's *Single Ladies*. People love your video!

Congratulations, the community validated you as an unintentional comedy genius. It wasn't exactly what you were going for, but the recognition is still nice. Certainly, this example is the exception and not the rule, but it's happened before.

For a second, let's consider that your video did not go viral and the overwhelming number of people who watched it didn't care for it. I would still consider this a success. You didn't let fear keep you from doing something you wanted to try.

Whether participating in an analog setting or a digital realm, we need to learn to accept our failures and filter the criticisms that come along with those failures. So what? Some random person on the Internet said your dance looked like a sweaty, disabled penguin. Maybe they have a point and maybe they don't, but it's your job to absorb those criticisms and decide what to do with them. Some critiques may be particularly harsh, but they also may be incredibly accurate.

When I was working on my senior project for my undergraduate degree, Professor Bertozzi told me my initial idea was horrible and I needed to start over. She didn't mince words, but you know what, she was right. I totally revamped the project and went on to create an award winning video game campaign.

Negative criticism and constructive criticism can both be utilized to your advantage. What can't be utilized is baseless criticism. If someone is spewing toxic at you just for participating, then their viewpoints are not welcome.

It's true, words can hurt, but like Eleanor Roosevelt said, "No one can make you feel inferior without your consent."

Lastly, I recommend supporting causes you feel strongly about. As my colleague Diana put it, "I'm a big advocate for advocating."

One issue that I feel strongly about is net neutrality. Net neutrality is the idea that internet service providers and governments treat all network data the same. In other words, net neutrality maintains an equal playing field on the internet. To learn more about net neutrality and its potentially monumental impacts on your life, visit:

http://www.savetheinternet.com/net-neutrality

There are tons of different causes you can support. One great way to find and connect with people that may share the same passion that you do is to visit change.org

Your participation as an online citizen is many things. It's creation, it's research, it's critiquing, it's filtering, it's supporting and most of all, it's important.

You are an absolutely crucial ingredient to the decadent marinara sauce known as the online community. Without you, what is arguably man's greatest achievement, is nothing.

Chapter 4 practical recommendations:

1. Don't let fear stifle your creativity. Create a song, video, forum post, research idea, experiment, photograph, business project, drawing or whatever and share it.

2. Share solutions that you have found to problems and enhance the online community by asking additional questions.

3. Be mindful when critiquing others. Ask yourself if your critiques can be beneficial. If not, keep them to yourself.

4. Don't feel defeated by criticisms of your work. Absorb the useful ones and use them to improve and disregard the extraneous ones.

5. Get involved with or start a cause that you feel strongly about.

CHAPTER 5: YOUR KNOWLEDGE - CONTINUING EDUCATION

Research has shown that communities in the U.S. with the lowest percentage of substance abuse, teen pregnancy, DUI, imprisonment, rape, robbery, etc. are those whose citizens are the most educated.

Education raises society as a whole. Granted, I do teach college so my views already lean pro-education, but I'm not referring only to higher ed. The more opportunities we seek and experiences we have, the more well rounded we become.

It makes sense, exposure erodes ignorance. Everything we know and do functions on a comparison to experiences we have had. In its simplest terms, the more comparisons we are able to make, the more educated and reasonable conclusions we arrive at. Experience softens the intellectual

Bell Curve.

Online experience also has its merit. At our fingertips we have greatest repository of knowledge the world has ever known and it's our duty to assimilate it like the Borg from *Star Trek*. Certainly, not all sources of information are worthy of our time, be they online or otherwise, but another important part of our job is to filter out the noise.

So how does one filter out the noise? It seems like everyone on the Internet disagrees which certainly makes coming to a conclusion more difficult. I find that participating in the community is one of the best ways to develop our personal truths. Ask a bunch of questions and field a lot of answers. Then, take those answers and blend them into a malted milkshake of confusion. I find that sauntering around with a head full of slush eventually results in a personal truth of at least soft serve consistency. Once you get to that point, go back and report your findings. Wash. Rinse. Repeat.

Education comes in many forms. Traditional schooling certainly counts. Traveling counts. Work counts. Socializing counts. Several years ago, I was chit chatting with my sister in her room. Her bedroom featured a large trunk positioned up against one of the walls. I decided to take a seat on that trunk as we continued our conversation. A few minutes into the discussion, I got a weird feeling on my back side and I noticed an unfamiliar odor in the air. As it turns out, that weird feeling was heat and that unfamiliar odor was burning cotton. What I had failed to notice prior to sitting, is that I was sharing that trunk with a lit candle. So, yeah, the time I lit my tush on fire, that was certainly an education. Whatever route you choose, seek out as many experiences as you can.

My education began in preschool. I was fortunate enough to get a full ride on a hop scotch scholarship. I can't name one specific thing that I learned in preschool, but after the initial shock of Dad dropping me off in a strange place with people I didn't know, (Apparently Dad did not take Mom's stranger danger talk as seriously as I did.) I can say it made it easier to be away from Mom and Dad for small segments of time. I was very much a homebody as a child. I wasn't shy by any stretch of the imagination, but I was most content at home with my family.

Kindergarten has been one of the most valuable educational experiences of my life. I learned about love. My buddy Josie let my best friend, Brett, know of her intent to marry him. In my six-year-old mind, that gave me the impression that the girl just tells the guy "we are getting married" and that's that. As it turns out, that's not that far from the truth. Beyond forceful marriage, I learned the essentials. Things like sharing, thinking positive, respecting one another and empathy. You know that saying "everything I need to know I learned in kindergarten?" I actually believe that there is at least a nugget of truth to that expression. We live in a world with a lot of obstacles, but one of the biggest obstacles we face is often ourselves. When things get tough, fall back on those lessons from kindergarten, you'll be surprised at how useful they can be.

Grades 1-12 were pretty standard fare for me. I learned a ton, but like most students, I had very little interest in being there. My most memorable subject of study throughout my high school years was my independent study on female biology. Bazinga! In any event, my teenage year escapades could likely serve as the topic of a book all their own. Some things are perhaps best left unwritten.

Even when I first started college, I didn't have the drive or passion necessary to complete it. My first major was a two year track for pre-med. A course of study that featured lots of science classes which prepared students to complete a bachelor's of science degree and go on to grad school. My priorities remained relatively consistent. I wanted to party with my buddies and chase girls. While college can be a great place to do the aforementioned activities, it also requires the dedication to study.

Even with my poorly organized list of priorities, I still did relatively well in my classes. The problem was, I had no idea what I wanted to do with my life. Mom always told me to be a doctor when I grew up, hence the initial start in pre-med. My passion really lied with technology, though. I decided that college was for suckers, so I dropped out to get into the work force. As it turns out, this was one of the best educational decisions I ever made.

In case you have never tried, getting a decent job without some kind of post secondary training is nigh impossible. I looked all over the place and was lucky enough to find a position. It was hard work. It was a dirty, thankless job with long hours and grouchy customers and I got paid very little to do it. I did, however learn a lot.

I envisioned myself staying in that position for 30 years and the thought was very depressing. I also pictured myself leaving and trying to find another position. Of course, I would just be trading one low wage job for another. The thing that really sealed the deal for me was the idea of having no opportunity for growth. No matter where I worked, without some kind of higher education, I was going to be the exploited grunt.

Reality is truly a fine instructor. Instead of my parents and counselors telling me that I should go to college, I came to the conclusion myself. I just happened to do it the hard way. I've always believed that finding out what you don't want to do is equally as important as finding out what you do want to do.

Since I was positive that I didn't want to work in high stress, low wage jobs for the rest of my life, I enrolled in college and haven't looked back since. Whether college is in your future or not, capitalize on as many learning opportunities as you are able. I've found that they can often offer fun and potentially prosperous side paths on our journey through life.

On a practical side note, I remember always being told to find something I like and pursue it for a living. I'm going to go on record and officially say that is horrible advice.

Here are a few reasons why:

1. The minute you start exchanging money for doing something you love is the minute you stop loving it.

2. It's very likely that what you love is not a viable business.

3. Many people don't work in the field in which they major; particularly if the major is not skill/trade based.

I think better advice would be:

1. Find something that you love. If you want to major in it, find a school that offers that program. Preferably, choose a local, low cost option if at all possible.

2. Double major in something very practical or skill based such as nursing/accounting/IT if it's a tech college plumber/electrician or another trade may be an option.

3. Find a good paying job that you can stand. If it's a job you love and it's secure, you win!

4. Continue doing what you love as a hobby in your spare time.

5. If you have a steady income and you want to try and turn your passion into a business, start part time while bankrolling the business from your secure job.

I'm a little bit of a weirdo. I'm just a naturally curious person. I've enjoyed studying in several areas like real estate, psychology, insurance, IT, the ways of The Force, The Power of Grayskull, etc. What I've found is that the more I learn, the more I realize that I don't know. It sounds defeating, but it's incredibly exciting. All of us have access to more knowledge than we'll ever be able to consume in one lifetime. We no longer have an excuse to be bored.

Your creation and consumption of resources is vital to a more educated community and the rewards that come along with it. Online universities, wiki's, blogs, social networks, video sharing sites, they are all your digital crops chock full of binary knowledge ripe for the picking!

Regardless of your path, promise yourself that you will never stop learning. Never stop growing. Never stop opening your mind to new ideas and forming educated personal truths. There are no excuses for your ignorance anymore. You're not just a local citizen of your district, you're a citizen of this globally connected world.

You are, Citizen 2.0.

Chapter 5 practical recommendations:

1. Online citizenship starts with analog lessons. Make time to learn how to appropriately socialize and interact in-person and transfer that etiquette online. Go to a cocktail party and mingle!

2. It can be difficult to escape our digital world, but make time in your schedule to be away from electronics. One of my favorite things to do is take my dogs for walks.

3. Share your experiences; they are invaluable to our human condition.

4. Be a problem solver! When you identify an issue, go a step further and offer solutions.

5. Never stop learning. We are counting on you, Citizen 2.0.

ABOUT THE AUTHOR

C. Ethan Blue teaches Information Technology at Nicolet College. He is a part time real estate investor, author and musician. His interests include education, business, computer technology, sports, movies, music, video games and animals. He may be contacted at Citizen2.0@cebcorps.com

www.ingramcontent.com/pod-product-compliance
Lightning Source LLC
Chambersburg PA
CBHW041143050326
40689CB00001B/460